MY TALK BOOK TWO

As your light shine on me, I feel pain
No joy
Only sorrow

As I think of my life, I want to hate you; loathe you for my pain and suffering, but I can't.

I have to hold on to you because I know a better tomorrow comes.

I know you are there for me and with me no matter the storm and storms that come my way.
I have to endure because you are beside me.

You are my right and left hand.
You are my joy and sorrow; pain.
You are in my life and a part of my life.

Michelle and Michelle Jean

It's March 27, 2015 and I am seeing many things that scare me. My eyes are open yes, but I am scared because I am seeing more water disasters and I cannot tell you which country is going to get hit. Hence death is masking death; keeping death from me.

Dear God, I am weary and troubled because I am all alone in this. I have no one to turn to but you.

This morning I dreamt I was on the sea and or somewhere at sea. The water was rough, but not rough to the point where you could not swim in it if you are an adrenaline junkie. For normal people you could not swim in these waters lest you be swept away.

Seeing the rough water I could not get off the island and or the land I was on at sea. I eventually got to safety as my sister's husband had a rope that he tied to a log or tree – something to lead people to safety. I got to safety along with his children. He made sure his children were safe.

Getting to dry land he told me the earth was cracked. So because the earth was cracked and or gearing up for an earthquake the water was rough. Reaching safety his children and I ended up in this apartment building that was like a hospital. There were people in the building and this lady was getting ready to give birth. The white nurse that was medium built had to go and assist her.

Yes this is weird because this is not the first time I am dreaming about sea devastation. It's been happening a lot lately but I just can't remember the full extent of the dreams.

I also dreamt my brother in LA. I dreamt we were in court and we got this black judge and or official. He presided over my brother's case. He had all the evidence for which my brother was not guilty, he was innocent. But the judge brought up something to do with his son and him spanking and or hitting his son and I gasped; made this sound because I did not know he did that. Well, suffice it to say the black judge and or official did not go further with the case. The case was put off for another day. My brother was not pleased hence he said something about he should not have carried me. Wow this is like when I was there in LA and we had our tiff, and I told him I wished I never came to LA.

So yes I am getting bit in the ass in the dream with what my brother said. Back on board. Like I said the case was put off for January 31. I said to the Judge and or black official, January 31 already went and he said something about March 31, but in my head I am thinking February. But I am pretty sure he said March 31. On this day I should come back and he will drop everything. People, I don't know but this man took a liking to me and he kept smiling at me, but at the end of the dream he had his arm around this other woman as he left. My brother and

I left also because he said he was hungry. So because he was hungry, we went to this Jamaican store to buy patties and bread. He bought a box of patties and bread and one of the clerks took the bread and patties as if carrying it to his car. So we did not get the bread and patties in our hand. Also in the dream they had these fudgesicle like ice cream. Now people this is where it gets odd because I wanted a fudgesicle and I wanted one of the employee (Shebada) to steal the fudgesicle for me. Hence I truly do not like this dream, so I have to wonder if Shebi (Keith Ramsay) is going to come out with a movie and or play that involve stealing. I also don't know if someone is going to come and steal from my brother again. There are so many factors involved hence I have to truly watch this dream.

Destruction, destruction because humanity is going to feel it real soon.

Children are going to be hurt; cry and moan because the wickedness of man has gone on for far too long.

<u>**I know time is winding down for me Good God. I know you truly want me to be in the Cayman Islands, but I cannot go without funds and you know this.**</u>

I know it's imperative for me to go there, but if you are not opening financial doors for me in a good and true way in the living and spiritual world, how can I get to where you need me to be?

How can I buy you your 25 million dollar mega mansion? If I have no financial resources or means, how can I accomplish what you need me to do for you?

I have nowhere to go. No one to say, hey, Good God needs a 25 million dollar mega mansion can you help me financially. And I refuse to put myself in debt further because of you. You cannot see my financial need and continue ignoring me. You cannot say you need something and not give me proper tools to get it for you.

You know what she did.

You knew the hurt and pain it would cause me and yes you, but yet you permitted it anyway. So how can I help you when the wicked and evil has and have made me financially helpless, broken and penniless?

My complaints are not getting through, so what do I truly do?

How do I continue to help you if you continue to allow others to truly hurt me and take all from me?

True life isn't about hurt and pain, it's about good and true living, and if the God that you more than truly and unconditionally truly love cannot see this and truly shut down all that is wicked and evil; all that causes his children and people pain, what good are you to them including me?

Yes you are the source and there is so much you can do, I comprehend this, but what about us, the needy; those that truly need you? You are our life, so why dessert us?

Why leave us alone to face the storms of evil; wicked and evil people including spirits alone?

Go back to Fred Hammond's Total Praise. Are you not our total praise; my total praise?

Are you not the one we look to for strength and healing? So let the evils of this earth and the spiritual realm be done now come on now.

We need a good change Good God, and without you we cannot have this.

<u>We need you and we should not have to fight with evil to get to you or have you. No one should. We are coming to you then clear the pathway and let us walk true to you. Come on now.</u>

There is so much that I need from you, but yet you are telling me no in so many ways. So how can anyone continue to walk with you if we feel abandoned and broken by you?

Why should anyone yearn you to the point of insanity?

Why should anyone fight evil to keep you if you are their true and unconditional love?

You love us so, then truly love us so then. Give us the true you so that we can overcome all that is wicked and evil and live.

We truly need to live.
I am looking to you for you then look to me and your true people also. You know that you are our rescue then truly rescue us.

I keep seeing water, and the waters of life are gearing up to abandon wicked and evil life and I am scared. Like I said, I know you want and need me in the Cayman Islands, but I cannot get there without funds. I am more than financially broken. I am in debt, so truly help me to get out of it.

Truly help me to help you in a good and true way. You know that my greatest fear is losing you and here I am scared because I see the waters of life and they are roaring. Evil has to go and I will not stop this because everyone is tired Good God. We all need that which is wicked and evil to go right away. True peace and harmony must reign supreme now.

You gave so many of us the goodness of you and they've used it for evil; wickedness, and I truly cannot do this because you are more than important to me. Losing you is not an option, but yet the hurt and pain is too great in my life right now.

There are days when I want to hold you as a human but I can't.

There are days when I just need you to be that overprotective father in the flesh but can't have you.

There are days that I need your true love. Need you to say you truly love me, but I can't have this and I truly don't know why? Yes I know cleanliness but why should this stop you from telling me you truly love me. There are ways you can do this but yet you fail to do this for me. Remember Blackman Redemption World Cry - Christine Lewis. Did you not relay to me a message for her? So why can't you tell me you truly love me and you will always be with me?

Sometimes being married to you Lovey is not enough. We want to be told frequently you truly love us.

Lead by example come on now. See how I tell you of my true love for you in different ways, well you need to do it too. And don't tell me about energy and spirit because I know for a fact that spirit and energy can and do love; you said you loved us so, so truly don't go there on this day. Yes I know the magnitude of loving us so, but I am a true lover, loving true and unconditionally; hence I am the greater and better lover. Smile because I am not testing your truth on this day. I just wanted to say that because you know it's true and this is me. Well to me anyway. You are a great lover too. Hey, you are better than me because you give wicked and evil people a home. If it was up to me they would all be gone; hence I petition you so much to separate us because I cannot take wicked and evil anymore.

Good God, why do we have to feel hurt and pain when it comes to you?

Why do we have to fight for you?
Why should anyone ward off and fight evil to get to you?

Why do we have to yearn and cry so much for you? You see the tears and pain but yet you do not help us to ease it; ease our pain.

You know our desire but for once can't you desire us; desire to be with us in the flesh that much?

Why can't you let everything be okay?

Yes I am in tears because it should not have to be this way. Why should we want you so much to the point of going insane and you don't want us; can't deliver us?

We need you but you don't need us. Why should this be?

Yes I see the raging waters. But Lovey why can't your good and true people find you now?

Why do we have to wait so long to attain and achieve you?

Yes I am hurt and in pain, including crying whilst writing this book. Hence I look to you for all including strength.

Death is masking death hence humanity is going to more than cry shortly. Ah Lovey, I truly don't know anymore because nowhere is safe.

Lovey my son and his friends are going to Cuba shortly and I am asking you to secure them and let them be safe in all that they do. Keep them for me Good God because I am depending on you for all.

Truly watch over them because you know the way I am with you when it comes to my children. I over love them as some of us Jamaican's would say, and please don't say ya think because you know it's true.

Keep Cuba safe because I know the waters of life is furious; gaining strength and fury as well as gearing up to take human and animal life on a massive scale real soon.

Yes the tears are gone because I took the dog for a walk and I am feeling better. I am also listening to Total Praise by Fred Hammond.

Oh Lord – Good God, I have to thank you because you are there for me no matter my pitfalls and tears; pain and sorrow. No matter how I lash out at you, you listen. Now I am listening to Fred Hammond's **THANK YOU LORD FOR BEING THERE FOR ME.** Good God if only we could truly thank you like this and feel good; hence the tears are coming again and I truly thank you for all that you've done for me yet again.

Good God truly thank you for being you because I more than need you. I truly need you in my life and can't do without you. You are more than my Total Praise, *so truly* **PLEASE DON'T PASS ME BY. I MORE THAN NEED YOU BECAUSE YOU ARE MY LORD, MY GOD AND KING. YOU ARE MY FATHER HENCE I COME TO YOU WITH ALL.**

Good God, I have all to lose hence I can't lose you. If I lose you, I would have lost all. I am not looking to Jesus Good

God, I am looking to you Good God and Allelujah and you know this. You know my tears, fears and feel of you, so touch me and hold on to me as I hold on to you. Please don't let me go, but dry my tears because today I am weak.

Today I want to continue on, but I cannot continue on without you. I cannot continue alone. I need to know you are truly there with me and for me.

Please take away my fears because the time for evil to go down is now, and I cannot get caught up and wrapped up in evil. Things are happening in my life and I have press on despite my setbacks and pain.

You are my truth hence I am hanging on to you. You know the battle and trials I face, and I have to face them alone but I cannot succeed without you. I cannot succeed alone. Truly hold my hand and be my feet; the true feet I need in life. Be my true financial resources and reservoir in life; the living and in the spiritual realm; world.

Heal me because the spirit is broken; scared and I truly don't want to be scared no more.

I know you are my glory and the Cayman Islands is where you need me to be but I cannot get there without you. I know I have to get there but how can I get there without your financial help.

You cannot say you need but yet do not give me the tools to succeed. Lovey, I can't walk alone in life anymore because it does hurt, and it does hurt my spirit. I know you are my rescue but remember yesterday, how I hurt someone hence I wrote these:

Why is there pain in life?
Why do we hurt others?
Why do I have to battle with my emotions?

No I do not want to hurt anymore.
I do not want to cause others pain, but how do you prevent this without causing you emotional distress; turmoil?

Should we live to please others all the time Good God without falling apart? I mean you're not living for you; you're living for someone else, and that's not fair to you as a person and or individual.
Good God, how do I stop this hurting?
How do I stop me from hurting?

How do I live with myself after hurting someone?
How do I escape into oblivion?
How do I escape into another world?

My life is not right nor is it fair.
I am in pain but you cannot see this; you cannot help me to live again.

How do I ease my pain and come out of this lonely and depressed life?

Is this the life you want for me Good God?
Is pain and hurt what you truly want for me?

I can't run from the hurt and pain anymore.
I can run from myself.

Dear God why me?
Why choose me to feel such hurt and pain?

What say you to me when my life isn't truly clean; I feel pain?

Good God, Lovey, why can't things be more than infinitely easy for me?

Lovey, why can't you take away all my pain?

Michelle and Michelle Jean
March 26, 2015

Why me?
Why him?
Why did I have to hurt him?

Why couldn't I have lied to him?
But lying is not me, but yet I did hurt him; could not give him what he wanted.

He did try, but I could not be with him; could not give him his heart's desire. Hence I hurt him; caused him pain.

Am I sad?
Yes I am sad.
Sad I hurt him.

Sad that I could not make him the one I wanted; but in truth we were not meant to be. He was not ordained for me nor were we compatible.

The strength I needed and need I cannot find in him.

The comfort level I needed and need was so not there. Hence I cannot force myself to be with someone I truly do not like in that way.

Friendship is important to me and if I am not attached to you sexually then you and I cannot be. Hence my spirit cried. Truly did not want to be with him.

I could not lie to myself.
I could not lie to my spirit.
Him

I have to be true to me.
I also have to stop hurting myself with S2.

I have to move on for the betterment and sanity of me.
I cannot continue to let others hurt me and lie to me. I have to do better for self and not take my hurt and pain and hurt others.

This is not fair to me nor is it fair to anyone; him.

Michelle and Michelle Jean
March 26, 2015

When I need strength who do I turn to Good God?
Who do I stretch my hands to?

In all you see and know, you see my pain and hurt and continue to neglect and reject me.

My life isn't the same anymore because there are days when I can't carry on.

My life is being hindered.
My full potential down.

I cannot keep praying to you for help and true help does not come when it comes to leaving my kids and moving on.

It's either them or me hence I choose me. Choose life because I truly can't live with them anymore.

I need my sanity.
Need my life.

But with all this said Good God, why are you ignoring me?
Why are you not truly helping me?

You see my hurt and pain but yet you say who cares.
Yes this is how I feel. You know what she did to me but yet you have not vindicated me.

You know what he did to me but have you vindicated me? Yes with him you did, but what about her? Truly vindicate me because she was wrong to hurt me.

Good God why?
Why do you permit such evil?

Why do you allow others to hurt people so?

Good God I truly don't know.

All I know is my life is not right nor is it safe, but yet you refuse to lift me up in a good and true way.

Allelujah, is this going to continually be my life? A life of hardship, unhappiness and pain?

Lovey, Allelujah, is this your master plan for me?

Please tell me now so I can let go.

Michelle and Michelle Jean
March 27, 2015

Lovey I am listening to **YOU ARE EVERYTHING TO ME by Fred Hammond** but I do not have to tell you that you are everything to me because by now you should know this. But just in case you've forgotten, <u>**know that YOU ARE EVERYTHING TO ME.**</u> You are more than precious. Yes I know time, your time and the time of man but with knowing this, Lovey, it does not ease my hurt and pain.

Do you truly know my truth and true love of thee?
Do you know what it means for someone to tell you that you are everything to them?

Do you know the fullness and goodness of me when it comes to you?

Do you know the purity of heart that I have for you?

You are my world and I don't want to lose you, but yet at times I feel as if I am losing you.

I feel unimportant to you because I am so emotional when it comes to you.

It's like all to me is you and it is, but yet you make me feel something is missing between me and you. It's like I feel hindered when it comes to you at times, and I truly don't know why despite what she has done to me. Good God you are my every day. So why can't I be your everyday each and every day?

Truly loving you should not be this hard for me, but yet it is and it should not be. If you are there for us then ease my pain, ease the pain of your good and true people. No one should live in uncertainty and pain when it comes to you. You should not be pain and or painful.

I know you don't want it this way, but it is Good God. Hence we look to you for everything. I do.

I am tired of the pain Lovey. Truly tired of it because I've lived my life in pain. Ever since I was young until now I've lived in pain. Why can't it stop now?

I am broken and I am crying out to you but you've ignored me. I've told you I can't walk alone anymore. I can't take this lonely and depressive road anymore. I've devoted myself in goodness and truth to you, dedicated my children and the good and true seeds you've given me to goodness, cleanliness, honesty and truth of you but yet it's not enough with you.

What else is there Lovey?

What more can I give to you of me before I fall down and die?

What more can I give you if I have nothing else to give?

I am broken, but yet you cannot see this. You cannot see and hear my complaints to you.

I've given you everything but yet it feels like I've given you nothing.

I am weary but yet in all of my weariness, you can't take my hand and say Michelle all is going to be okay.

In all of my weariness you cannot say, all is well between me and you; our good and true people.

In all of my weariness you cannot provide a good planet; home for me and your good and true people, including the environment of earth.

I know the pain and struggles of this earth Good God. I know her pain but yet you allow evil to rein; devour and kill her. Yes I know your pain, but yet you continue to live in pain. We can no longer hurt others because of our pain Lovey, it's wrong and we both know it.

Lovey look at Mama Africa and see how tired she is. She too is weary but yet with all this said, I am the one she reached out to and not you. Why?

You are King; All. She should come directly to you but instead she needed prayer from me. I know you do not feel away but this should not be, she should have come to you and you should truly protect your own from sin; the sins of man; wicked and evil people and spirit.

Look at the waters Lovey and tell me the way man is destroying it, if it is necessary; right?

You mean everything to a lot of people Lovey, so truly save them and not ignore them like you do me. Yes evil is for a time but what about our time with you?

What about the time of Good, when do we get our turn?

What about your true glory and goodness Good God, when does this time come?

We need to hold your hand and hold on to you, but yet you do not give this to us.

Look at our hurt and pain and tell me if searching for you constantly and continually is fair?

We've become wanderers and vagabond looking for you. We can't find you in a world that is riddled with sin and hate; evil; pain.

We've become nothing, reduced to beggars and thieves; murderers in societies that praise death; the devil. Truly list to EVERYTHING TO ME by Fred Hammond and tell me if our living is fair to you. You are our strength and healer; all, but yet we are so weak. We as your children and people feel broken and abandoned by you.

Truly tell me, you are going to do something about this.

Tell me something, if you continue to leave us alone will we not continue to do evil things?

Will we not continue to live in sin?

Will we not continue to choose wickedness and evil things including people and spirits over you?

Tell me, if you are everything to me, why am I not everything to you?

Why should I feel lost and alone; abandoned because of you; truly loving you?

Why should anyone feel this way?

You cannot continue to lock us out because we are knocking your door down and you cannot keep it shut. Something has to give. You can't say you need truth and when you get it you can't handle it; you abandon it.

Lovey if you are everything to us then be everything to us. Truth is not one sided, so truly do your part to help your own because we've reached critical mass and we have to get out of Babylon lest we be destroyed; devoured; go down in flames like them. Come on now.

So as I dedicate EVERYTHING TO ME by Fred Hammond to you, truly listen to the song and lyrics and truly be my everything. Know that you are truly needed in my life. You are important to me.

Michelle and Michelle Jean
March 27, 2015

Ah yes, it's been a teary day for me and as the pressure and pain come yet again in the form of bills and reduced funds, I accept them and walk alone as always. I know one day I will overcome; I will rise and be totally debt free. Yes Good God and Allelujah, in your name and your name only, I claim my victory over my financial stresses and pain; woes.

I claim victory over the stresses my children give me.
I claim victory in your name Good God and Allelujah over all my enemies here on earth and in the spiritual realm; including those enemies that have not yet risen.

I am free because she is dead and she can't hurt me anymore. She's in rotting. So in all I do, I thank you Good God and Allelujah. You are my Lord and King always.

Yes single motherhood is a bum bum but I have to go through it. I have to face my burdens alone and do what I can eventually to fix them. It's a pity I could not upload this collection bill to this book and show you what I have to go through. The nastiness of some collection agency, but one day Good God, one day, it will all be over because I will overcome; you would have given me the victory over them where I don't have to deal with them ever again. I claim my right and victory with you Good God; hence I look to you for everything. You are my laughter and pain; hence I am leaning on you right now for comfort and truth; victory always.

You know the truth Good God. After paying Rogers Fido all that I've owed them on a delinquent cell service that was used by my son, they are telling me that I now owe them $216+ plus interest via a collection agency because I refuse to pay the bill.

Yes I refuse to pay the bill because service was cut from you and the phone service was cancelled in June of 2014. I have the original cancellation number on file. No one told you to reactivate this service. But because you were told on the 25th of July to put the bill in my son's name while delinquent bill was in credit and collections you took it upon yourself to reactivate the phone. A phone that was not being used. And yes I have confirmation from you that this change was done (the bill would be transferred to my son's name). Now in February of 2015 you are sending me an email saying I owe you this amount of money when I've cleared up my debt with you. Why should I pay you a cent more if I am not using your phone and you were the ones to take it upon yourself to reactivate the phone without my consent? You were told to transfer the bill to my son's name only, nothing else and this was confirmed by you. And yes someone in your office had the gaul to say I called in and told you to reactivate the phone. Why the hell would I do that if the phone number has been transferred by my son to another phone company? I am not the one using the phone and I take it upon myself to call you to reactivate it without telling my son.

How stupid would I be?

How stupid are you? Two different phone companies cannot share the same phone and or cell number to my knowledge, so don't you dare tell lies on me.

But you know what Good God, Rogers Fido can do all they want. I am tired of cell phone companies that rip people off in any way they can whilst telling lies on the person.

Right now I truly don't care nor do I give a damn if they report my name to the Credit Bureau because I've had it.

<u>*This is why I do not have a cell phone for myself nor do I want or need one anymore. I've been through enough with them because of my children. I'm already broken so add this one to the list of brokenness that I cannot fix right away.*</u>

Add this one to the list of worries and troubles that I come to you for.

Add it all because I have kids stress, health stress, financial woes and stress, physical stress, spiritual stress, loneliness stress, emotional stress. Just keep them coming because ALL I HAVE TO SAY IS, IS THAT ALL YOU GOT. KEEP THEM COMING BECAUSE I AM FED UP NOW.

Fed up of being broken!!! There is so much I can take before I keel over and die. I am spiritually and physically bankrupt. Truly bankrupt, hence I have nothing more to give. I am looking for death to come knocking at my door again and then I am gone. I cannot take anymore. I can't man come on now. Why me? I truly can't take no more, truly can't and you're not listening to me.

Why me? Why me?

Why me?

You see my stress and heartache but yet the things I need help in you cannot help me.

My life is surrounded by sin; evil but yet you are okay with this.

What the hell have I done you to warrant such pain?

What the hell have I done for you to leave me alone in this way?

I've given all that there is to give of me but yet pain and suffering still surrounds me. SO CONTINUE TO GIVE ALL YOU GOT GOOD GOD. CONTINUE TO HURT ME AND WALK AWAY FROM ME BECAUSE I WILL NOT FALL ANYMORE. I TRULY LOVE YOU MORE THAN UNCONDITIONALLY.

I REFUSE TO GIVE UP ON YOU EVEN IF YOU'VE GIVEN UP ON ME. I AM ROCKED YES, BUT ROCKING ME DOES NOT MEAN I AM GOING TO STOP TRULY LOVING YOU.

I WILL NOT FALL BECAUSE YOU CANNOT TRULY ME, YOU CAN ONLY LOVE SO.

So keep the hurt and pain coming because there is only so much I can take before I die like I said.

Life means something to me. Maybe it means nothing to you, but it does mean something to me. Hence I am still living despite my health and financial woes and concerns.

Remember we are not just physical beings we are spiritual beings and when I walk away from you we will truly be done. Yes I gave you my word and I will honour my word to you but I truly do not have to honour it in the spiritual. And yes this is wrong of me to say this because you have my unconditional truth physically and spiritually. I truly more than over love you, but you cannot continue to let people cheat others unfairly. I paid you off. You reactivated my contract after I've paid you. No, when I have money I will pay Rogers Fido. I will no longer fight with Rogers Fido for justice. So go ahead Total Credit Recovery and let this affect my credit because I care not anymore for man's unfair and thieving system. I owe you, I owe you. I will pay you slowly until you are paid off again Rogers Fido. Hence I refuse to have a cell phone. All when I am broken down in the dessert I want none. I would rather walk till mi drop dung from dehydration than have a cell phone with any murderous and thieving phone company that deal in unfair and thieving practices.

No cell phone company is worth the bullshit that they put their customers through. So because I have none, no cell phone, I will truly do without.

I have a LAN line and it's going to stay this way. Pay phones are there and if I can walk to get to one then so be it. **This is why I tell you Good God and Allelujah, no one should come in and take one cent of the money I put away for your land and lands including true people. I will not have anyone cheat us of what rightfully belongs to us. What I put away for us is not based on thievery, it's based off and on truth and true love. I've made you my unconditional and everything and it should stay this way more than forever ever without end.**

You are my desire and destiny, so why would I not want and need to protect you and all that you've given me.

I have no true friends apart from you hence I tell you everything. I come to you with my hurt and pain.

I cherish you and all you've given me, so why would I not keep you and all that you've given me clean, good and true?

I do not play humanities dirty little games. What and who I truly love, I cherish, spoil and keep near and truly dear to me. I've told you, my greatest fear is losing you and you know this. So keep coming with the stress because like I've said, I can only go so much before I keep over and die.

Man is unfair I know this, but if this is what we have to continuously live with, why choose you at all? Yes I know man has and have created law and laws to aid the wicked and evil. But what about the just that's trying to live fairly; clean, so that they can one day reside and or live with you?

Man create law and laws to kill hence I create none. I refuse to. Life is true and truth must reign forever ever without end real soon.

All that is wicked and evil must come tumbling down infinitely and indefinitely forever ever real soon, so I

worry not about wicked and evil companies, societies, financial institutions, hospitals, whorehouses, homes, churches, synagogues, mosques, grocery stores, restaurants, people and spirits including animals.

So truly, is that all you got. Keep it coming because hey it will be another messenger bites the dust when it comes to you and the true you, but I refuse to be because of you and or when it comes to you.

Preserve goodness and truth because all I have is goodness and truth for you come on now.

Preserve kindness because kindness is in me for you.

I'm tired Lovey and you know this. I can't handle any more stress because my body and spirit is weak. So do all and take all that is wicked and evil from me and around me. Do all to take my stress, financial woes and pain including health woes and pain from me. Yes I was meant to end up in the streets, but I cannot end up in the streets because of them. I am a fighter in many ways but I truly cannot fight anymore I am truly tired.

My spirit is tired. I need to rest from all of this heartache and pain for awhile.

Please, truly stop the pain because I have nothing left. All that's left for me now is death, and soon death will be at my doorstep and trust me I will not fight him. I will go with him, but rest assured you will never be with me in the spiritual realm because you see the evils of man and let them continue robbing and hurting people including me.

So don't tell me about loving so because LOVING SO CAN NEVER BE LOVING TRUE IN MY BOOK.

24000 years you've allotted to evil. Each member of the council of death had a thousand years each to inflict hurt and pain upon your people. Now I ask you, when is enough enough with you?

Was this right and justified?

And yes I am sorry for questioning you like this but you know my anger, the anger of your people. Lovey, we lost it all and now look at us. Yes I know this is what we get for abandoning you, but am I abandoning you? <u>I cannot love you so, because truth is the greatest gift of all in my book, and I do truly love you more than unconditionally.</u> You gave me the gift of truth and true love and I cannot abandon this for death even though I want death to come because of heartache and pain.

And this is also because I feel helpless on this day. I need you, I need you, I need you and cannot have you the way I need you physically and spiritually. Lovey all this heartache and pain should never manifest in man again come on now.

Our world, kingdom of truth and true love should have no heartache and pain in it whatsoever Lovey.

Lovey I am looking for this on earth right now so that I can stick my tongue out at wicked and evil people and say, Abay, you lost and Good God won. I know this is my cheeky nature but Good God and Allelujah, why can't your people including me have this now? Have your true peace here on earth right now.

You know we cannot face the hardships anymore. We are giving way and dying. Billions have accepted death because the pain and suffering is too great.

Now tell me, for all those who have taken their life because they could not go, who's going to save them?

Are you going to save and redeem them?
What goodness are you going to bestow on them?

How can you look at them and tell them because you've taken your life in the living, you must go to hell?

Now I ask you, how fair are you in all of this?
Have many not come to you in the living for a saving grace and none was given?

How many are like me that have and has cried tears to you; told you that they cannot take anymore, but yet you continue to let them suffer at the hands of evil. How can they truly forgive you for their hurt and pain? They came to you because they could not withstand anyone suffering and pain.

They came to you for a saving grace.

Ah Lovey, let me stop because my mind just told me you were not the God of their choice.

Yes I forgave you for what she has done to me, but I will never forgive her for what she did to me. This is my right, hence there is no forgive in me to give for her and to her. She did me wrong and she did cause me pain. Yes you allowed this, but I forgive you because you are deserving of forgiveness. You've been there for me despite my anger and pain. You've never failed me in anything.

But Good God, (yes this is me and it's not what now) go back to the days of old and those crying babies that were fed to Alligators. Black babies Good God. They were fed alive by wicked and evil people. Now I ask you, do you expect them (these babies) to forgive you?

How can they forgive you knowing the way they died at the hands of evil; wicked and evil people?

Now look at the seas, waterways; life and original life and tell me, how can the waterways forgive you for all that humanity; man has done to destroy and pollute it; kill it so that it becomes uninhabitable?

Like I said, you are everything to me hence you are my pain and joy, my happiness and sorrow. I have to come to you with all in this way and more. Truly forgive me of my wrongs when it comes to you Lovey, but I have to get you to think. I have to get you to answer me so that I can answer them when they come to me.

You have to look at your people and tell me if heartache and pain is what you truly want for them.

Look to those that truly love you more than life itself unconditionally and tell them why you truly hate them.

Tell the why you are not truly there for them.
Tell them why you prefer evil over them.

No don't cry. We are in pain.

The road is rough and tough.

Our life is filled with many pitfalls; pain. The suffering can't go on anymore come on now man. You are our everything but yet you continue to let us live in pain for what?

Are you not our right?
Are you not our good choice?
You're my good choice, so chin up because I know my victory comes. But we cannot continue to suffer at the hands of wicked and evil people and spirits; corporations that think not of the betterment of humanity but the betterment of self; self greed.

Lovey I truly do not want or need to be like this. I need you but I refuse to call up on Jesus because Jesus is death; dead to me.

I need life; you, so why can't the life; good and true life I need come from you? You are my keep so continue to continuously keep me and your good and true family.

Truly let all be well with you and us.

Ah Lovey, my cup over flows each and every day. Maybe one day all will be well between me and you where I do not have to write to you in this way.

Maybe one day I will see you face to face in human form and when I do, trust me I am so going to pinch you and let you feel my pain and sufferings despite you being in the storm and storms with me.

Yes you are my destiny hence you are my cure for all despite me lashing out at you in this way. Everything takes time with you because I know spiritual time is not the same as physical time. Earthy and or spiritual time must catch up to spiritual time in time. But one day you will be mine and I am so looking forward to this day.

Truly stay cool and be all that I need in all that I do.

You are my good all, hence you are everything to me.

Michelle and Michelle Jean

Further and before I go, I have found the perfect song by Fred Hammond called, **BREATHE INTO ME OH LORD.** This song is ideal for me and you because we all need your true breath of life. If we had your true breath of life we would truly be whole and right with you.

ALSO YOU HAVE TO LET EVERYONE GLOBALLY KNOW WITHOUT A SHADOW OF A DOUBT THAT BELIEF CAN NEVER EVER, INFINITELY AND INDEFINITELY NEVER EVER GET THEM INTO YOUR KINGDOM AND ABODE. TRUTH IS WHAT GETS THEM IN BECAUSE TRUTH IS EVERLASTING AND ETERNAL LIFE.

ANYONE CAN BELIEVE IN YOU, BUT IT'S NOT EVERYONE THAT TRULY KNOWS YOU.

FAITH ALONE CAN NEVER GET ANYONE INTO YOUR ABODE EITHER. YOU CAN HAVE FAITH BUT WITHOUT TRUTH AND KNOWLEDGE WHAT GOOD IS FAITH?

Come on Lovey, humanity need the full truth of you, so give it to them come on now.

Lovey let me be frank with you. Yes, yes I know I am frank with you all the time, but belief is BULLSHIT IN MY BOOK COME ON NOW.

Lovey, look at the different religions of the globe and how many have and has converted from this religion to that religion because of belief. Billions say they believe in you and as soon as someone comes along and give them fool's gold, religion, how many of them jump ship; abandon you and say they've converted to this religion and that religion. Hence it's a fool that takes religion to you and think that they are safe, going to get into your kingdom and or abode.

Religion isn't peaceful nor is it of you, so why the hell would I want something that deceives me when it comes to you?

Like I said, my greatest fear is losing you, so why would I accept something or someone that takes me from you come on now?

Lovey, look at how I quarrel with you and shed tears.

Look at how I truly love you beyond anything known and unknown to man and the universe.

With you I can be weird because I always tell you the truth and trust me this was not easy for me and you. I've come a long way with you and I'm still challenging you and your true and good will. Not because I am defiant but because I need you to think and do right and good by your good and true people. So no, I will not put faith above truth, because truth is all that I know and want to know. Yes I know lies; death, but you are the Breathe of Life so why would I want anyone or any other God a part from you.

Can another God lift up my spirit when I am down.

Will another god take my abuse? I trust you above all hence my truth and troubles is you. I get more than I can bare and I can dumb on you and lash out at you with them. I've done this above. Like I've said in some of my other books, I would rather come to you than go to man and do something stupid. Man give wrong advice but

you don't. You will always give me the right answer after I am calm.

Look at it, after telling you off and cussing you, I found BREATHE INTO ME OH LORD by Fred Hammond and Michael Bethany. Good God, I found this beautiful song and I truly thank you because I do need you to breathe into me your good and true breathe of life.

Without you we are dead but humanity fail to realize this. We've been lied to and we continue to accept these lies.

Why can't you be our good worship and praise always? Why can't we truly lift our hand and hands to you and be satisfied with you in all that we do?

We've been used and abused by religion. Lovey, look how many children are crying to you in pain because they're molested by members of the clergy.

**Look how many are on drugs.
Look at the suicide rate and death rate due to religion and tell me if this is what man truly kills self for?**

Religion brainwash people and this is what you want for your good and true people including me?

I am out and I give you thanks for taking me out. No one wants the truth of you much less you gave me a gift that they want. Wow, Allelujah you saved me and I truly thank you.

Why the hell would I want to go to hell because of religion and the uncleanliness of religion?

Religion teaches murder and hate and I truly do not want this for us and our people Allelujah.

I need your breath of life to be with me always in goodness and in truth. You are our cleanliness hence no other god will do.

I need to be clean and pure by your standards and my standards so that I can truly live and or reside with you forever ever, so why would I continue to taint myself now that I know the truth?

Yes I know if we do not accept you, you will leave us alone to our choosing and this you have done to billions then and today.

You take my blunt force because I do not know better; do not have a better way to vent.

Lovey you are my all, my doubt, my question and questions because I do question you, so why would I not want and need to be whole with you?

Lovey you've blessed this man with a brilliant voice that I cherish. Ah Lovey, if only I can or could perfect my voice so that I could sing beautiful melodies like this. Trust me if I could, I would have you in tears of joy and praise.

Lovey we are looking to you for all, hence I truly don't want or need you to disappoint us. Too much has happened Lovey, too much and I truly need it to stop.

You cannot continue to allow evil to destroy it all. No evil can do good because the good that they think they do is looked upon as evil and it is evil. Evil do to get even if it's a tax receipt and or tax write off. There are always conditions when it comes to the gift of man. Trust me if the rich man did not get a tax write off or receipt he would not give; do. They do to get even if it's a place with you. **Think it not because it's a fool that thinks I do to get a place with Good God. I have one with him already, and trust me I am looking to build him our good home including universe.**

In this day and time Lovey, the gift of true giving is rare hence humanity and or man can never comprehend me and you and the way we live; our living.

You are my saving grace no matter what, and no matter my yoyo emotions and unbalanced emotions, never forget you are the one for me; you are truly rare. So I got you; have your back; all.

I know many things I have to go through, but the loneliness gets to me. Like I said, at times I need your shoulder to lean on and I cannot have this; get this.

Lovey this isn't fair to me or anyone that is journeying to you and with you. Why should we be hindered come on now?

You see my pain and anguish of not having you to hold. But yet I cannot comprehend why things have to be this way between me and you.

I cannot comprehend why we have to be kept from you.

Good God I seek justice for me and my life.
I seek justice for our people.

Lovey I will not stop telling you about the babies; black babies that were fed alive to alligators.

I will not stop asking you if you heard their cries and tears because you see mine; my cries and my yearning for you and of you.

I will not stop asking you, how this made you feel?

These were babies Good God, but yet you did not save them, you made death take them brutally.

Look at the pictures of some of our black ancestors, how they were sold into slavery by our evil own. **Look at the brutality they faced at the hands of wicked and evil demons that lived and still lives in the flesh.**

Lovey when I see the pictures of my people, our people in chains, how am I to feel knowing how wicked humans are to each other? Demons walk and live amongst us I know because we keep letting them in, but when does it stop? Why can't we infinitely and indefinitely stop them in the living forever ever without end?

Look at the killings and massacre that's going on right now and tell me, what is life worth to man, when man kill each other for a place in hell?

Tell me something Lovey, are you burdened by these things?

You said you love us so, but yet man kill each other and take from you.

As the Breath of Life, (Allelujah), how can you live with yourself knowing and seeing the ills that humans do daily; each and every day?

How can you look upon a wicked and evil person that knowingly destroy and kill and say I forgive you?

Babies Lovey, children died brutally and you are telling me that you are okay with this?

Look at what I am going through and tell me if you are okay with this?

Lovey many of us are single mothers trying to raise our children right but failing miserably at it like me. I am ready to leave my children and go to a next country where I can be by myself.

Lovey I need cleanliness; you, but I cannot have it in the environment I am in, and each day I stay here I want and need to leave; go.

Good God you need to prepare a way for your good and true people because you are our good worship.

You are our good all, so why are you truly failing us?

Am I missing something Good God?

Please let me know because it's not fair for your good and true people including me to live without you.

It is not fair for your good and true people to go without you. You are our living, so why are you allowing wicked and evil people to take you from us?

Like I've said, why can't you be our total praise?

Why should our praise and worship be tainted by evil?
<u>Why should our praise and worship go unanswered due to the sins and evils of our surroundings globally?</u>

Why should evil command us and have us doing his and her dirty and unclean will?

You are clean Lovey, so why can't we have your good and true; clean will?

You are our right like I've said, so why do you continue to allow our right, You to be taken from us?

Humanity can keep religion; the religions of death. As long as I have you, I am more than okay come on now.

Yes I can let everything else go, but I refuse to let you go.

Michelle and Michelle Jean

So in all that you do Good God, thank you for Fred Hammond and his beautiful voice.

Thank you for giving him the gift of music.
Thank you for the song BREATHE INTO ME OH LORD. Hear what he said, <u>*"breathe into me oh Lord the breath of life, so that my spirit would be whole and my soul made right. Breathe into me oh Lord every day so that my heart is pure before you always."*</u>

Tell me something Lovey, who would not want this for self? Just the thought of you make me want and need this continually. I need to be pure and clean with you.

Lovey and Family, Good God knows the way I am with him hence I am more than fierce when it comes to him. I know I have to go through turmoil. I know I have to be strong with him hence I am this way. <u>IF I UNCONDITIONALLY TRULY LOVE YOU, LET ME DO ALL THE GOOD THAT I CAN FOR YOU. JUST AS HOW GOOD GOD WANT AND NEED TO GIVE YOU OF HIM UNCONDITIONALLY LET HIM. LET HIM HEAL YOU FINANCIALLY. LET HIM HEAL YOU PHYSICALLY AND SPIRITUALLY. HE IS THE BREATH OF LIFE, SO LET HIM GIVE YOU OF HIM ALWAYS. THIS IS WHAT HE WANTS BUT OUR EVIL WILL AS WELL AS WICKED AND EVIL PEOPLE (RELIGION) BLOCK HIM FROM DOING SO.</u>

Listen Good God is there for you continually.

People and Family it's not about money, it's about truth and true love. Good God truly loves us and we need to truly love him. It's not fair for him to be giving of him constantly and we give him nothing back. He does get burnt out and yes in many ways this is why he has left us to our will; the god and gods we choose and chose for self.

Please don't look at my financial constraints; my finances will no longer be an issue soon. I know he is going to lift me up in his glory. Yes I am hurt, but I can't go to anyone else but him because he truly knows my pain. With him I am different and I truly need it to stay this way.

He's my breath of life; hence I call him Allelujah; Good God and Allelujah, Lovey, Darling, Baby and yes Lord and King. I cannot call him by any other name because I cherish him beyond universally.

People do you know how wonderful unconditional love of truth is? Sweetie, my family, let this song BREATHE INTO ME OH LORD SPEAK FOR ME NOW. FIND OUT WHAT TRUTH AND TRUE LOVE IS. THIS SONG TELLS YOU

EVERYTHING WE NEED TO KNOW ABOUT PURITY AND TRUTH ON THIS DAY. *I am sure there are many songs out there but I cannot give up on Mr. Fred Hammond, I have to gush about him because pure hands and a clean heart say a lot. People and family I cannot let anyone take my Lovey from me.*

My hurt and pain he feels as well. Do you not think he Good God does not cry?

He does.

- Our sins make him cannot come to us.
- Our sins take him away from us.
- Our sins make him leave us.
- Our sins make him divorce us.
- Our sins make death laugh at him.
- Our sins put him to shame.
- Our sins tell him Good God and Allelujah that we don't want and need him; we don't care.

- Our sins condemn us and in a way condemn him because we've become unclean; sinful in his sight and the sight of man. Come on now. Rise up and let go your sins. Oh Allelujah, praise your holy and wonderful name. Yes Lord, praise your holy and wonderful name because you are more than worthy to be praised. Allelujah. Oh Allelujah all the praise is due to you always.

We are the ones hindering him. I need to put my head on his shoulders and tell him face to face that I am proud of him. I am truly proud of him, but I don't want to tell him in writing alone, I need to tell him face to face. I more than truly love him and I refuse to let anyone take him from me. So whenever possible I have to dedicate music to him. I need him to have my praise and words of truth.

Know that you can have him too. Yes you can.

Like I've said, let no one tell you that your good deeds can't get you to Good God.

Let me tell you something, Oh Allelujah, praise your holy name. Goodness and mercy will always follow you if you do good. HE GOOD GOD AND ALLELUJAH IS OUR GOODNESS AND MERCY AND HE WILL ALWAYS BE WITH HIS PEOPLE NO MATTER WHAT.

Yes I question him and I know those little yiddy babies who were fed to Alligators so many years ago are vindicated. All who hurt them is burning in hell right now. This is why I tell you, I worry not about wicked and evil people. **THERE IS A APP FOR WICKEDNESS AND**

EVIL INCLUDING OUR SINS AND THAT APP IS HELL.

I've told you the reason why we cannot hear wicked and evil halla, cry worse than a bitch in heat in hell is because there is so much noise around us.

I've told you, I would never ever forgive her for tying me. She tied me so that I would have nothing in life. She was hindering me from doing the work of Good God. Now that she is dead, she is seeking my forgiveness in jail; hell. No I cannot in good faith or true good will forgive her because she broke me more than financially. She did all to take my true love from me and I truly cannot forgive her for this. I will never ever forgive her for this because it was not me alone she hurt. She hurt Lovey also and he did not deserve it. She broke me man come on now. I did not have to cuss him so reckless and rude. I did not have to cuss him to the point where I wanted him to kill me. No one deserves this. I still cuss Good God for the betterment of his people yes. And yes you can say I disrespect him, but in truth I truly don't. I am an impatient one when it comes to wickedness and evil. I want evil; all facets of sin and evil to be gone right away and he knows this.

People and family, there is a timeline of evil because evil got time to deceive. I cannot break this timeline I know this. The time of evil must fully come to an end and this is before 2032. I know this, so if you are not right with Good God and Allelujah, redeem yourself and make yourself right with him. Have that relationship with him.

Do not get caught up in evil because once the timeline of evil is up, Death have to take all who belongs to him on a massive scale globally.

Please truly listen. You read about Noah in the Illuminati Book of Death and or your Free Mason Bible of Death which is your so called holy bible. See what he went through, hence many died when the flood came. They did not believe him hence **THEY WERE LOCKED OUT OF GOOD GOD'S KINGDOM.**

The waters are here again. I see them raging, so if you are not right you are going to be swept away; die. This is no joke; disaster's I see and I let you know them. Every night I go to my bed I am being reminded of the United States of America. **The Exodus must begin for Good God's true people because life will not be the same in the West. Many black people are going to die because they accepted death.**

Yes I cuss the black race for us to wake up. I cuss them for them to stop worshipping the idol and idols of religion. Good God is not a religion and we cannot keep turning from him. It's time now to return home. We have to return home and if you are not with him you will be left behind. And trust me all that is left behind death will take violently.

LISTEN, IF A MAN AND OR COUNTRY; THE LAND YOU LIVE IN IS TREATING YOU UNFAIRLY, THEN WALK AWAY FROM THAT LAND. DO NOT STAY AND BUILD IT. DO NOT CONTINUE TO HURT YOURSELF.

Like I said, as blacks we complain about injustice, but yet are unjust to our own including Good God.

We complain about injustice but yet stay in unjust lands.

If a man or woman including child don't like me; do all to hurt me, I am going to find a good and true way to move away from him or her including that child. I refuse to stay or go where I am not wanted.

It's amazing how Good God has been trying to rescue black people and we keep slamming the door in his face literally.

Go back to your so called holy bible and read about how some of our ancestors got beatings brutal. Today is no different from then. **WE KEEP ACCEPTING THE IDOL AND IDOLS OF BABYLON AND WE GET BEATINGS FOR IT.** Stop being the beating stick of Babylon man come on now. Put these stinking and shitty idols down and find your God – Good God and Allelujah again.

Staying with your so called holy bible. Go back to Moses and how he went up into the mountain and when he came back he saw his people worshipping and or dancing around the golden cow or calf. Did not your book say the ground opened up and ate and or devoured those people? Well the earth is opening up again and billions will be devoured in this day and time because a greater flood comes. And like I said, if you are not right with Good God, Allelujah, then death is going to take you to hell with him; you are going to die. And if you think slavery was brutal, think again because the brutality in hell is far worse than what (all) blacks faced in slavery combined. If you think feeding little yiddy babies back then was evil, honey that's child's play compared to what your spirit is going to face in hell. I told you, your spirit is dependent on water and there is none in hell. There is no water in hell just spiritual fire. Once you are imprisoned in hell you cannot and will never get out. There is one way in and one way out and that way is death; death of spirit, then your spirit and or soul will be no more again.

But you get beatings?

Good God does not beat me; I beat up on him because I am surrounded by negative forces. Like I've told you, he's in the storm and storms with me. All that is happening to me is not due to him. **It wasn't him that tied me, evil tied me but I blame him for it.** I have to blame him because he's all I know and see each and every day. **I am not expecting him to let evil infiltrate our happy home in any way.** Don't think he's not shutting down evil. I have to go through this for you to see my pain and anger. I have to go through this so that when evil is shut down permanently and indefinitely forever ever no evil returns to our land and lands including within us.

I am setting the foundation and framework for the collapse of all wicked and evil systems infinitely and indefinitely forever ever without end everywhere. **I am setting the frameworks and foundations with him so that no form of evil and wickedness; sin infiltrate us ever again.** And yes this is also why she tied me. She knew who I was. I was death's intended target but death failed. Hence Lord, Good God and Allelujah, Lovey, sees my true heart's desire always.

Also Lovey, I have seen what drunkenness can do and I am truly asking you to add alcoholism and gambling to our portfolio of truth. HEAR ME ON THIS DAY, THE 28 OF MARCH 2015 AND NEVER EVER LET OUR CHILDREN AND PEOPLE FAVOUR ALCOHOL AND GAMBLING. Good God I am not saying they cannot drink or gamble, but never ever let any of them get drunk to the point where they hurt self and others. Good God I see what alcoholism can do and I am asking you to never ever let anyone in our family, land and lands favour alcohol and gambling. Lovey, this hurts, truly hurts hence you've seen my fear, pain and hurt when it comes to alcoholism.

Lovey, addiction is more than painful. Addiction destroys more than the family; it destroys the spirit, hence I truly beg of you to secure our good and true family when it comes to addiction of any kind. Lovey it's not right, it's not right, it hurts and this pain I truly cannot take or handle.

No one should have to hurt family and self when it comes to alcohol and drugs come on now. No one should have to hurt in any way when it comes to life. Pain is a bitch and you know I truly can't deal with pain.

Look at how I hurt this person and how I've been hurt. Hence I have to let go hurtful things. So because I hurt him I have to go back into my shell and not seek to get involved with anyone.

Yes I know I can't force myself to like or love someone in a way that I truly can't; but if hurting a person comes with the territory of love and true love, then I would truly rather stay to myself and not get involved. I truly do not like hurting anyone nor do I set out to hurt anyone, not even in these books.

I have to be true to you and myself Good God, and hurting anyone willingly or intentionally is not on my agenda of truth and never will be. **<u>Hence I've learnt that you cannot hurt others because someone hurt you.</u>** I know the cost of it hence I would rather walk alone with you than get involved with anyone.

You know family; I am so use to being by myself. I've been hurt all my life and as soon as I push my head a little out of my shell, I am hurt and ended up hurting someone. Yes I cried hence I have to be the true me. I have to live for my happiness and truth.

Am I funny and weird; strange?

Yes I am because your happiness means a lot to me. I would rather stay alone and walk alone if it means hurting you. I can't handle hurting anyone, this is not me. I've given into society and the bullshit of what we as humans do already. Right now I've found truth in my God and I don't want to let it go. In many ways I am happy but in others I am not. I am passionate about writing hence I write in this way as well. I need what's good and best for Good God's true people as well as him. I am more than passionate about you and when you choose to walk in the way of death it truly hurts me and it hurts Good God and Allelujah also. **We truly do not think of him, hence WE AS HUMANS AND HIS TRUE PEOPLE LET THE DEVIL'S PEOPLE TELL LIES ON HIM.**

HE DOES CRY AND FEEL PAIN. HE CAN'T TAKE OUR BULLSHIT ANYMORE AND THIS IS WHY HE'S LEFT US TO OUR CHOOSING. Listen, I am broken but with all my brokenness I am healed at the end of the day. Good God never leaves me in tears. Even if it's a song he gives it to me; meaning let me find it. I found Breathe Into Me Oh Lord by Fred Hammond and trust me this song has and have healed me in so many ways.

I needed food yesterday and I got food. Good God and Allelujah is good to me people. He's truly good to me. I am wanting and he does provide for me not matter how small that provision is. On the days I am truly weak, my pitbull Queenie will come and cuddle beside me or rests her head on my sofa chair. So I am not without true love. I have true love hence Queenie knows I truly love her.

I don't have to tell her I need affection she gives it to me.

Yes I want to leave my kids and go away because I need them to learn the hard way that if

someone truly loves you, cares about you and wants what's best for you, treat that person right because they are there for you no matter what. Do not let the devil come into your home and take your unconditional love of truth from you.

My mother has always been my unconditional love in the living. I did not realize just how much she truly loved me until when she died. In death she's protecting me because when death came to take me she was there holding my hand. And yes I know Lovey you are jealous but I cannot give up on you because you sent her to be my guide in the dark storm and storms that came my way. You are both my always, hence I more than love you both more than unconditionally.

I will defend you both because the both of you deserve it. I need the both of you in all that I do.

Yes I have financial and health cries; woes. She tied me so that I would have nothing and she's dead now and no forgiveness was allotted to her by me.

I will rise and my health woes will soon be gone, hence I have to claim my victory with Good God and Allelujah and yes my mother also because she too is there for me.

I know some of you are saying well that's not a lot, your provision is small. But for me and to me it's a lot because I was truly hungry and I got fed.

Hey, I needed a sofa because the one I had and was sleeping on was done for. My younger brother called me and asked me if I wanted a sofa and I told him yes. People and Family, I got a leather sofa and love seat that reclines. Now my feet won't swell up when I sit down and write for extended period of time and I can sleep great. Trust me I am so happy because my needs were taken care of. So in all that I do, I have to trust Good God and Allelujah because he is truly there for me and you.

Hey remember I bugged him for a vacation and my brother sent me the money to buy my ticket. The price was too high and I waited until the price came down and I was able to go to LA despite me not wanting to go. Yes LA opened up my eyes to certain things. **<u>Hence America needs to deal with their homelessness. It's a crying shame for a land that says they are a super power to have so much homeless living on the streets. When you are there you can feel the poverty; just how poor the land and or country is.</u>** Yes many people don't see or feel this poverty but I did. **<u>There is too much injustice in this land hence poverty will always surround them.</u>** You may not comprehend this, but look at their national debt of over 18 trillion dollars. This debt is draining the country of their riches and life; hence America is going to feel the wrath of death real soon literally.

So kids, let no one tell you to hurt the ones that truly love you. Learn to listen to good council. **AND DON'T YOU DARE SAY IT BECAUSE GOOD GOD HAD IT BRUTAL WITH ME WHEN IT COMES TO LISTENING. Trust me he held on to me tight and he's still holding on to me.**

We all have different issues in life I know, but the one thing that keeps me going is knowing that I will soon have peace and rest with him; life.

Let me tell you something at times I feel like Job in the book of sin; your so called holy bible but I am not him. I am Michelle, Michelle Jean; the female Lyon (Lyons).

Trust me Good God needs no one to kill for him. Death needs you to sin and kill so that he can take you to hell with him.

HEAR ME NOW; GOOD GOD NEEDS NO ONE TO KILL FOR HIM. DEATH NEEDS YOU TO SIN AND KILL SO THAT HE CAN TAKE YOU TO HELL WITH HIM.

Like I've said time and time again in some of my other books in the Michelle Jean series, truth does not hurt, lies hurt.

<u>**If Good God is shielding and protecting you, don't let him go for anyone including me. He is there with you already, so stop changing from him by accepting the religions and idols of death.**</u>

No one can make you clean except you.
No one can wash you like you.

If you need cleanliness and strength ask Good God to show you what to do. Yes we slip and fall but pick yourself up, dust yourself off and continue on your journey to him and with him.

<u>**Listen, the little he Good God does for us is great. He saw my need and needs and provided for me without me knowing and he can do the same for you. Yes it may take some time but give him the time he needs. He's been doing it for us so why can't we do it for him come on now?**</u>

I need to truly live people despite what I say above. I have to vent and do vent. Yes I want and *need everyone to know Good God and Allelujah, but it's not my choice to say choose him. He Good God and Allelujah has and have given me seeds in a brown paper bag to plant over 100 million acres, and it is these seeds I must take care of. It is these seeds that I must secure in goodness and in truth. So by me securing these seeds, I have to secure true happiness for them. I have to secure a good and true place for them with Good God and Allelujah. In doing so, I have to more than infinitely and indefinitely forever ever without end lock out all facets of sin and evil including death. Our kingdom and abodes; homes must be pure and clean. The children we now have must be pure and clean and walk in goodness and truth; cleanliness with him, with self, for him and self including the earth and universe. None must walk in sin and evil including hatred.*

No one that has a pure heart can hate based on skin colour. Yes I loathe and hate and I tell you and Good God of this and he's helped me. Hence I refuse to pick up arms to hurt anyone or against anyone.

I refuse to go to anyone's shaman or obeah man to hurt anyone. I can't do this. Let evil lay hence I vent in this way and you all know this. Like I said, I do not cuss the black race because of hate. I cuss them because I want and need them to wake up and save self. As humans we've forgotten how to listen.

Many of us have and has become ignorant.
We don't want to hear the truth; hence many have and has turned back the truth.

Many say they have the truth but all they have are lies, hence they preach and teach lies; deceit.

I refuse to be like them hence I am different; a little weird in some way.

Good God can't keep giving us the truth and we keep refusing him. He's fed up, I am fed up hence he's only going to save those who are true to him. Yes the true Jews. You refuse to listen and you keep walking in sin, so as you walk in sin, death must devour and consume you.

Yes as blacks our true heritage and true story was taken from us. (history)

- *Our language was taken from us.*
- *Our home was taken from us.*
- *Our god was taken from us.*
- *Our children were taken from us.*
- *We were beaten and brutalized.*

- *We were raped and sodomized.*
- *We were fed death.*
- *Beaten to accept death.*
- *We were condemned.*

Our culture was taken from us and we were given sin. But it's time we wake up and say no more. I have to go back to him, my good up good up Good God and Allelujah; true life and king.

We can no longer walk in disobedience and this is what Good God is trying to show us as well. We cannot continue to let him go.

People and Fam, we are getting a beating from sin's people and we still sit in it and take it. Good God has and have tried to save us, we are the ones to neglect and refuse him and this cannot continue to be this way. Something has to give and it is giving. You have to save self now and if you don't want to and or try to save you, it's all up to you because you are going to die. You cannot neglect Good God because he's tried. You cannot blame him for your death. You are the ones that keep refusing him by clinging to religion; death.

I know the mountain people and I've told you about it. Yes the mountain represents the messengers of Good God also. Meaning no matter how beautiful the mountain is, you have to go through sickness. Hence I've told you, when he Good God and Allelujah marries you, it's for "in sickness and in health and in death do you part." Meaning if we as messengers choose death and or willingly sin and deceive; He Good God and Allelujah does depart from you and leave you to death. Hence through death do you part.

This is our vow of truth and no one can change it. When Good God chooses you, you are married to him because he does put a wedding band on your finger in the spiritual realm. This is your band of truth and lifeline with him always.

Listen, we need to listen to Good God now. Know that he would never send anyone to deceive you or lie to you.

He would never send anyone to tell you to choose death because he is good and true life and I've told you this in my other books.

Good and true life must always be good and true and it is. It is man – humans that accept lies and pain and when evil beats us worse than a bitch, we cry out to Good God for help.

If he knows not you he cannot help you and will never help you in that way.

Like I said it's March 28, 2015 and I keep dreaming about the United States. This morning I dreamt about North America. I saw in blue this land so I Googled the map of North America to see if I could find the specific land I saw in blue with the exact shape and sure enough I found what I was looking for. On the map of North America the exact shape and size of the land turned out to be NV, Nevada. I cannot tell you anything else people and family. *I do not know if Nevada is going to be hit by a earthquake, but something powerful and strong is to happen. Blue is a powerful colour in the spiritual realm people.* Anyone that has this power can do a lot of damage to the spirit in the living and in the spiritual world. But in this case I cannot say because both good and evil use blue. So for me to see Nevada being outlined in blue say a lot to me.

I know something is to happen to the United States of America because my sleep world and or vision world is consumed by there.

Good God's people are being warned and it's time for the Exodus to begin for Good God's true and good people. The time has come my family for me to prepare a good and true place for you all with Good God.

The pain and suffering is almost over because Good God is truly with you. **You are his breath of life so let him live.** Put down the god and gods of Babylon and let's truly walk home. I do not and will never ever provide a home for the wicked and evil, hence Good God I am trusting you without a shadow of a doubt to not let any wicked and evil person or spirit including child follow us; walk with us to your glory.

You are our good light and way.

Michelle and Michelle Jean

Yes it's sad what's to come but we made it this way.

Like I said, I keep dreaming about water, sea water and I see myself on the sea and I truly don't know why.

Yes something is to happen to my family because my niece and son is provoking my dead family. I had to yell at my niece and kick out my son because I can't take it anymore with them.

My niece is going through a lot, but yet the story she's telling me does not add up. And for me to dream see my great grandfather that's been dead for decades is our wakeup call to start walking right and doing things right.

Fam, I did not see his face all I saw his feet. He was wearing black pants and yes I warned my niece. If she does not smarten up she is going to get seriously hurt. My great grandfather don't come out unless it's something bad; something that he cannot take. So woe be unto her and my son. He's a man that does not joke.

Family it's beyond me why any child that has a mother or father that truly loves them would walk in the way of sin and evil. Meaning do wrong things to cause your true loved ones pain.

Fam, I have to now change my tune with my second child and I do hope it's not short lived. I thought he was not hearing what I was drilling into his head, but by the Grace of Good God and Allelujah he listened.

I was shocked to hear the way he was talking. He and his friend was talking about realization and he said, he came to the realization of life and this is great.

He was counseling his younger brother on life. He told him, "my nigga learn from me, how mom had to push me to go to school. Get up and go to school, clean up your living area. If you do this mom would not have to complain." And he's right.

Go to school on time and do your chores. If you do this, what do I have to complain about?

If you have read any of my earlier books you will see how I complain about cleanliness, friends and school.

Have mercy Allelujah because I truly thank you. Bless you so much with goodness and truth. On this day, for the little I heard from my second child I thank you because he did tell me he would never listen to me. He has his life planned out.

Wow.

Truly wow because I saw a totally different side of him.

Lovey these children need to truly learn about good council. Lovey, I know listening is hard but these children need this so that they can live.

Life is given so why are they throwing it away?

If mommy and daddy say Joe stay come home right after school, go home right after school. I know some of you might want to hang out with friends but don't listen to them (your friends) tell you to disobey mom and dad. Listen to what mom and dad is trying to tell you.

Know that when you disobey your parent or parents, you won't feel it now. Just wait until you have children of your own. Trust me, you are going to feel it harder than the trouble you gave to your mom and dad.

And Dan stop laughing and saying I'm an idiot you are not going to have kids.

You might have step kids and trust me they will make your life a living hell.

And don't even go there, because if you have no step kids, you might end up in the wrong nursing home or hospital and trust me the treatment you get, you are going to wish for death literally.

Yes this treatment may not be at home, it could be you getting sick on vacation and get bad treatment. So yes, I know what I am talking out.

Hey you could marry a she or he demon and he or she treats you worse than shit. Trust me gold digger will have nothing on her because even yu yie ball shi nyam out to rawtid.

So kids, truly buckle down and do all the good that you can do to help your parents or parent in a good way. KNOW THAT DEATH KNOWS NO AGE LIMIT. IF DEATH HAS TO TAKE THE LITTLE YIDDY BIDDY BABY, DEATH WILL AND I'VE TOLD YOU THIS ABOVE WITH THE LITTLE YIDDY BABIES BEING FED TO ALLIGATORS ALIVE.

No, they did not do anything wrong and I cannot tell you what our ancestors did apart from disobeying Good God.

Good God's children were not to walk in the way and ways of the wicked but they did anyway.

Go back to Eve (Evening) in your so called holy bible. She disobeyed Good God and paid the ultimate price; death. She toiled in pain, conceived in pain and died a painful death all around. SHE LOST GOOD GOD AND NEVER GOT HIM BACK AGAIN. AND WE ARE NO DIFFERENT TODAY.

Let no one tell you someone is going to die for your sins and or die to redeem you from death. **ABSOLUTELY NO ONE CAN REDEEM YOU FROM DEATH IF HE OR SHE IS NOT ORDAINED TO DO SO.** *I've told you in my other books; female death is more powerful than male death. She does not like anyone standing in her way when she comes to take you. And don't think if you are a messenger of Good God she won't take you and the land you are in. She will because she is unstoppable when she comes.*

She does not give up her spoil or spoils when she comes.

Yes you can say I am a liar but know the truth because I am telling you the truth of what I saw.

KNOW THAT LIFE AND DEATH ARE TWO DIFFERENT THINGS AND IF YOU ACCEPT DEATH, THEN DEATH MUST TAKE YOU.

I've also told you in my other books that if you do not receive the upright eye in triangle you are doomed. Trust me if you get the downward eye in triangle, know for a surety that you are going down to hell.

I've told you who has their death certificate's already. Meaning their names are in the book of death and there is no way they can retrieve their names. (INSTRUCTIONS FOR DEATH).

So truly think because the life you save might be your own.

Life is about growth not death.

Life is about progression not regression and it's time we stop living like the regressed. Good God is not regressive nor does he like regressive people. Regression and regressive people keep you down. They burden you down because they don't want to move ahead in a good and positive way.

Know that Good God's triangle points up for a reason always, so look up to him and grow; live.

Michelle Jean

It's March 30, 2015 and I've overcome Good God. I've had to kick out my last child out and to be honest with you, I truly don't want him back into my home. It's time for me to leave, hence I am giving up my apartment by your grace and mercy so that we can go our separate ways.

<u>**I need this separation because I can no longer live in a whore house. I can no longer live unclean with my children. My life is worth something and I need to live.**</u>

What I am finding is that children want you as a parent to uphold and condone their slackness and I can no longer do this; condone slackness.

My children are not listening, so it's time for me to go because I have come to the end of the road with them. It's time for me to journey home. Just as you did to Eve (Evening), I have to do to them because good council is not with some of them and it's time they learn the hard way.

As parents we should not have to put up with slackness. <u>**The laws of man are slack and diseased.**</u> You have kids telling parents you can't beat me, if you do I will call the police on you. Well call the police because I am leaving your ass to rot. Rot in hell because there are no prodigal sons and daughters here anymore. *And no my son did not* say he was going to call the police on me. Once you're gone you are gone. I've learned a lot Good God and I've put up with a lot. I can no longer do this because I am the one hurting. Yes I want and need better for all my children, but if my children do not want or need better for self I have to let them go. I can no longer tax myself and tax you; hurt you in the process, it just cannot be anymore nor is it fair to you.

My son cannot see this and yes I gave him an ultimatum and he took it so he can never return home. I will not have it anymore with him. That child has and have put me through so much to the point of death, I cannot do this anymore. I am fed up and tired of the disrespect. I am tired of people; their friends and certain family members using my apartment as a whore house. I pay the rent but yet I have no bed to lay my head nor can I enjoy my home.

<u>I am fed up of me hurting and I am fed up of hurting you in the process. You do not deserve this. No parent deserves this come on now.</u>

Children, not all have become selfish and self absorbed. They think the world revolves around them.

Some, if they don't get their own way, they hurt self and this is bullshit. I've taken my children as far as I can go and now it's time for me to let go.

They need to grow by them self now. Yes I hate to let go but I have to let go for my own sanity; health. I am slowly dying and they cannot see this. My health has and have gotten so bad that I cannot go anymore. I am here in my home and I feel so weak that my body wants to drop, but I am fighting this. They don't know this. I've risked all of me including my health to feed and shelter them and I can no longer do this anymore. I have to live Good God. I can no longer journey with them and fight for them because some do not want good for self. The ambition is not there. Hence I refuse to let any of my children tell me bullshit about daddy was not there, this is why I did what I did. Have ambition because ambition goes a far; a long way. Soon the job market is going to get brutal. If you don't have a proper education what are you going to do? The welfare system of man will not be able to accommodate you, so think. Many of you will end up in the streets like the thousands that are on the streets of LA come on now. Secure your damn future. This is all mama wants and you are letting yourself down. You are not letting me down because I am on the last leg of my journey.

Mama is there and mama is trying to put you on the right road, you are the ones to choose the wrong road so don't blame mama for your lack of ambition and failures in life. I preach to unnu an teach unnu, a unnu nuh waan tek telling.

Don't blame the system for your lack of ambition and laziness as well as lazy mentality either. The system said, this is all I got; can offer; you were the ones to not get up on time to go to school and when you fail you say the teacher this and the teacher that. You did not study hence you failed self, you. You did not go to school hence you did not graduate, so blame no one else but you. You skipped class, did not do your assignments, so blame no one but you. You set yourself up for failure and you failed. Don't complain either when immigrants come and take the job that was meant for you. You got the tools to succeed and you were the one to choose to throw those tools away.

It is the same thing we do with and to GOOD GOD. HE GAVE US ALL THE TOOLS TO SUCCEED IN LIFE AND WE

ARE THE ONES TO THROW THOSE TOOLS AWAY AND EXPECT HIM TO PICK US UP WHEN WE FAIL.

HE SHOWED US WITH EVE (EVENING) THAT WHEN WE DON'T LISTEN TO HIM HE'S GOING TO LET US GO AND HE'S DONE THIS. WE CHOSE DEATH OVER HIM, SO LET DEATH TAKE CARE OF YOU BECAUSE ONCE YOU GO THROUGH THOSE DOORS YOU CAN NEVER COME BACK IN AND SO SAID SO DONE.

NOW WE BELIEVE IN THE BULLSHIT OF BLOOD. HUMANS ACCEPTED BLOOD; BLOOD SACRIFICES AND LOOK AT US TODAY, WALKING LIKE THE BLEEPING DEAD.

WE'VE BECOME LIKE SCAVENGERS PICKING AT THE DEAD CARCUS OF DEATH.

We believe in shit and do shit and expect Good God to accept the shit that we do and he cannot do this. Like I've said, billions did not choose him, hence billions are going to die.

We refuse good council like some of my children, so what they seek now is what they are going to get.

Yes I truly forgive them but I can no longer die with them. SHORTLY IT'S GOING TO GET WORSE FOR ALL GLOBALLY. AND LIKE I SAID, IF YOU ARE NOT RIGHT WITH GOOD GOD YOU ARE GOING TO DIE BECAUSE DEATH MUST TAKE YOU TO HELL WITH HIM.

DEATH IS GOING TO PUNISH YOU MORE THAN BRUTAL AND IT MATTERS NOT IF YOU DON'T BELIEVE IN GOD. YOU ARE STILL GOING TO DIE BECAUSE YOUR SINS OUTWEIGH YOUR GOOD.

I refuse to paint a pretty picture when the picture that man has and faces is more than butt ugly.

I've tried with my children. I did not fail them, they failed self because they could not learn; listen.

Yes I am dreaming and I will not decipher them anymore. I truly cannot comprehend my dream world and or what my dreams and or visions are telling me.

Dreamt this black man but I cannot tell you what he was telling me or said to me. All I know was that he made this juice of multicolour; beautiful orangey colour. He filled up the glass but I did not get the juice I woke up out of my sleep.

Dreamt my mother and she had short hair. She was driving me somewhere. I was in the backseat of her car. I can't remember if it was my daughter or son that was in the front seat. All I know is that we were going somewhere and she was driving fast. In her car she fiddling to open the roof. She managed to open the roof. When she did, she looked up at the sky; the sun. People the light that came in and or that I saw in the sky was so beautiful. Also in the dream I thought we would get to our destination at 8 o'clock pm, but from her looking at the sky she said, we were going to get there at 10pm at night. Our destination was Montreal. Like I said, she was going fast and thought she was going to crash into the bend. I think I told her she was going too fast and she slowed down around the bend. Ahead of us was water, dirty water because the rain came and the place; road was flooded out. I told her she was not going to make it through the water with her car because there was so much water, but she sped up and made it through the dirty water without the car shutting off. We came to this region where a cop was directing traffic and to the way the road was set, washed out, I thought she was going to hit the cop but she didn't. We made it to safety. Many cars were driving and you could see so many people at the bus stop waiting for the bus. This one black lady with her son decided to jay walk with her son and this man in a black SUV sped up and almost hit her and her son. She had to quickly retreat back to the bus stop before the SUV hit her.

Taking me to this place with beautiful buildings, I said to her because it's just the two of us now. I told her, I wish I could buy here one of these homes for her to live in.

I know my son is planning to go to Montreal after his Cuba trip, so I have to warn him; caution him to be careful.

Family, I have not seen my mother in a long time so seeing her is good. I like when she comes around me. I also know that when you dream see old death, it's new death. Someone in my family is going to die again. And because I've retreated in my shell yet again, I won't call my family and tell them; warn them.

I know my father is ill because my brother called me. He was with him and my brother told me I have to visit him more often with the kids. My brother wants me to go see him Easter Sunday but knowing me I will not go.

Yes my father was complaining that we don't come around him but family, if a man was not truly there for you when you were growing up, how can you be there for him in old age?

Like I've said in another book, I had to watch my aunt cuss him because I needed help and he would not help me. Fam, I WILL FOREVER TELL EVERYONE THAT IF MY FATHER DIES, I WOULD RATHER GO SIT AT MY MOTHER'S GRAVE AND TALK TO HER RATHER THAN GO TO HIS FUNERAL.

I am extremely funny and if I set my mind against you, you can never ever get me to come your way.

Like I've said, no child should be without a father and mother. This is why I get down on Good God too. Why should I be without him? I need him in all that I do.

I need him in my life to guide and protect me. I need to be safe in life and with him so yes I get down on him because at times I feel abandoned and no child should feel this way.

Many fathers here on earth has and have abandoned their children and when they get to old age they say they want their children around them.

Some hit you with the honour your father and mother bullshit. If you were never there for me why the hell should I be there for you? You let me go, I know you not, so why now that you are old I should step up

to the plate and help you; be there for you? My mother faced your bullshit, she honoured you by taking you out of your environment and gave you a better one and you could not honour her. I needed help when he died and in death, she was with me. She stayed my death when he came to kill me. You were not there for me hence I honour her and Good God and Allelujah. He sent her to keep me safe hence I will always honour and give them the praise. I will also petition him Good God and Allelujah to never ever condemn and or sin any child that cannot lend a helping hand to a mother or father that has and have abandoned them in life because they were not man or woman enough to take care of their own.

You cannot say you are a father or mother and abandon your child. You are not a mother or father you're a nobody that is

not deserving of anything in live. You are not deserving of the true love of your child. You abandoned them, mama tried with them, hence mama and Good God is due the praise come on now. I watched my mother try with us. She instilled education in us. She instilled goodness in us, what the hell did you do?

In her dying state she was helping me by babysitting my children, so yes in all that I do in life that is good and true, I have to honour her and save her always because I remember goodness. In death she did not abandon me. Hence I glorify her and Good God because they were with me and still with me.

When I needed them most they were there for me, so I will never ever give up on them.

I will not disgrace them by taking up religions of men anymore. I've put death down and taken up life and I have to live and honour them. I have to praise them because life is more than worth it, Allelujah, Good God and Allelujah and my mother is worth it.

Like I've said, if you have true love do not give it up for anyone or anything no matter the storm and storms that come your way.

I've faced hell here on earth and I refuse to die to go face a wussera hell come on now. I know what hell looks like and I'm to die and go there?

Stupid isn't written and or stamped on my forehead. I yearn and crave Lovey, Good God and Allelujah to the point where I feel as if I am going to go insane and I'm to leave him for death? I know what he's done for me hence I have to stand by him in pride and hold his hand.

Mi nuh wutliss.
Mi nuh ungrateful even if I seem that way to you.

I will not abandon him because of my hardships. Yes sometimes I want and need to, and I tell him this, but I am stuck to him more than crazy glue because I am that crazy for him.

People mi a get good food and I'm to give up good food for genetically modified crap? Hell no!!

My good up good up God and more than true and unconditional love is organic, so why would I choose inorganic over him come on now?

Go back to the song BREATHE INTO ME OH LORD by Fred Hammond and tell me if you of yourself do not want and need his breath of life?

Allelujah is the name we call out. We call out to the BREATH OF LIFE, SO WHY WOULD I NOT WANT AND NEED HIS BREATH EACH AND EVERY DAY?

I am the way I am with him because this is my choice. He is my choice of truth. I found him and I refuse wholeheartedly for anyone to come and take him from me. I found him and I've dumped everything that I have on him. He's done his job in helping me because she is dead now and now I can rise in goodness and in truth with him.

She made me suffer hence she is now suffering in hell and rightfully so. Hence I've told you time and time again in my other books, that if I am the saving grace of humanity, I will never ever safe anyone that is wicked and evil because they know the evils, ills and wickedness they have done.

No one should have to suffer because of wicked and evil people come on now.

Demons walk and talk hence demons are in the flesh. They are also humans. I know this and I am to accept death to go to hell and see this again?

<u>Keep hell and death. I will cling to Lovey all the way because I know the strength and keep I have in him.</u> **<u>Like I've said, if I could design a earth and universe that is based on total and pure truth and true love that is void of all sins and evil, hatred and wickedness, I would just for him.</u>**

I am not like you, hence I am different. He's with me and inside of me, and I'm to let him go after facing hell and still facing hell here on earth. No.

I would be ungrateful to him and I cannot be this way.

<u>I will not buy into the bullshit of society and the church anymore. No one should sell you death come on now.</u>

Good God never gave us any religion to take us to hell but yet we say, his only son died for us.

If he only HAD ONE SON, WHAT ABOUT YOU AND ME?

More importantly, why would HE GOOD GOD AND ALLELUJAH SEND HIS ONLY SON TO DIE FOR WICKED AND EVIL PEOPLE? IM NUH LOVE IM PICKNEY DEN. IM HATE (8) IM PICKNEY.

<u>*Let me tell you something, I would never ever send any of my children to fight on the battlefield of death to save wicked and evil people and children including spirits.*</u>

<u>**I know for a fact that Good God and Allelujah will and would never ever send any of his children (messengers) to go on the battlefield of death to fight and die for wicked and evil people.**</u>

Good God a nuh puppunennay.

<u>Good God is not your lying stick, so stop telling lies on him.</u>

No one can die to save you, you have to save yourself because that person did not sin for you, you sinned for yourself. Why should I or anyone lose their life to save you? You are wicked and evil and I'm to give up my life for you? Who yu? Your life is not more important than mine. I have my burdens to bare face yours.

KNOW THIS, DEATH CANNOT TAKE YOUR NAME OUT OF THE BOOK OF DEATH, SO WHY DO YOU THINK SOMEONE CAN DIE TO SAVE YOU.

FROM YU NAME GUH INNA DI BOOK OF DEATH, YOUR NAME REMAINS THERE. YOUR GOODNESS MUST OUTWEIGH YOUR SINS. IF YOUR GOODNESS OUTWEIGHS YOUR SINS, DEATH CANNOT HOLD YOU GUILTY OF ANYTHING BECAUSE YOU'VE MADE AMENDS FOR YOUR SINS COME ON NOW. GLORY ALLELUJAH.

So stop fooling yourself by thinking otherwise.

Your life is important, so stop letting wicked and evil people carry you to hell with them.

Wicked people don't want to be alone when they are dying. No, that's not right. Evil's job is to take and or eliminate all that is good, and this is why wicked and evil people do all to destroy and kill it all including you.

Good must not have life or access to Good God and Allelujah, and this is why evil people and spirits give you dirty water to drink, unclean meat and or food to eat.

They give you lust and all manner of fornication to keep you drawn and enslaved. Meaning they give you these things for you to try them, and once you try them your name is put in the book of death. You sinned hence that's 24000 years plus in hell for that one sin in the living. Now add another 24000 plus years in the spirit because we are both physical and spiritual beings. So for that **one sin** you are looking at 48000 plus years in hell and like I've told you in another book, death will not let your serve your time in spiritual time, he is going to make you serve your time in physical time because it was in the physical you did your crime; sin. And yes if you commit that one sin a hundred times, multiply that 48000 plus years by 100. So imagine how many sins you have on death's slate; book. Know that spiritual time is way in time hence the physical must catch up to the spiritual at a time in time and or a moment in time. Meaning if goodness is ordained for you, once physical time reach spiritual time in time your goodness is bestowed unto you. This is why many say God is slow, but God – Good God is not slow, we're just not on the same time nor are we in the same time zone as him. And yes, hence the different time zones here on earth.

Everything was left in place to find it, we are the ones that let others tell us to look in this direction and that direction. You can go to Good God directly, so go to him with your issues like I do.

Like I've said, he's not the one to fail us. We are the ones to fail him and we do fail him.

No one is ordained to die but because of sin, our flesh must go back to the earth for worms to eat it. All that is left of you is your bones; hence we are like unto dry bones. (Elijah)

Flesh and spirit was to go back to Good God whole but this cannot happen due to sin. We have to separate self and go to him in another way and this is sad.

Cleanliness is imperative; hence if you are not clean, truly don't go trying to knock down his door because you will never find him.

Well I'm not going to get there you say. Stop right now. Take a shower, sit up in your chair, sit on your bed, lay upright on your bed, stand in the shower, sit on your toilet, whilst standing and doing the dishes open up a conversation to Good God and Allelujah. If you don't know how to talk to him, tell him the truth. Tell him you don't know how to talk to him. Tell him you are scared because you are not sure of him, sure of what to do. As long as you are totally honest and true to him and with him he will help you.

He is there for you. Take baby steps to him.

I feel unclean so I can't talk to him. I don't want to take a shower because I don't have a shower.

So!!

I said, as long as you are truthful and honest with him. Tell him you are sorry you do not have a shower and cannot bathe. Remember we are both physical and spiritual.

WHAT YOU CANNOT DO IN THE PHYSICAL THE SPIRIT CAN DO.

BUT, BUT.

THERE ARE NO BUT BUTS.

YOUR TRUTH TO GOOD GOD AND ALLELUJAH CAN AND DOES WASH YOUR SPIRIT CLEAN IN A CERTAIN WAY.

Trust me, when you begin to have that connection with Good God you will begin to smell yourself. Your spirit will let you know that you need a shower. I know because this happens to me.

Sometimes all I want to do is write and I do and when the spirit cannot take enough it will let me know to get up and go bathe and or shower.

So rely on Good God and rely on your spirit as well. Know that this takes time. Sometimes you will fall but get up, dust yourself off and go again.

<u>Good God is not a monster; he's your true father.</u> He is there with you. Like I said, when I get angry at times and when I am calm, he gives me what I need to heal me. Trust me I found this song, BREATHE INTO ME OH LORD AND OTHERS AND I'VE SHARED THEM WITH YOU IN THIS BOOK.

I gush about Fred Hammond because I've found music I WANT TO DANCE TO GOOD GOD AND ALLELUJAH WITH.

Yes you heard me; read right. I want to dance with Good God and this song is one of the songs I want to dance with him to. (BREATHE INTO ME OH LORD)

Yes I am weird and you are thinking me to be crazy but it matters not what you think. As long as I have him I am more than good to go. Hence I am totally different from you and I more than infinitely and indefinitely forever ever cherish and care about him more than you.

Michelle and Michelle Jean

OTHER BOOKS BY MICHELLE JEAN

Blackman Redemption – The Fall of Michelle Jean
Blackman Redemption – After the Fall Apology
Blackman Redemption – World Cry – Christine Lewis
Blackman Redemption
Blackman Redemption – The Rise and Fall of Jamaica
Blackman Redemption – The War of Israel
Blackman Redemption – The Way I Speak to God
Blackman Redemption – A Little Talk With Man
Blackman Redemption – The Den of Thieves
Blackman Redemption – The Death of Jamaica
Blackman Redemption – Happy Mother's Day
Blackman Redemption – The Death of Faith
Blackman Redemption – The War of Religion
Blackman Redemption – The Death of Russia
Blackman Redemption – The Truth
Blackman Redemption – Spiritual War
Blackman Redemption – The Youths
Blackman Redemption – Black Man Where Is Your God?

The New Book of Life
The New Book of Life – A Cry For The Children
The New Book of Life – Judgement
The New Book of Life – Love Bound
The New Book of Life – Me
The New Book of Life – Life

Just One of Those Days
Book Two – Just One of Those Days
Just One of Those Days – Book Three The Way I Feel
Just One of Those Days – Book Four

The Days I Am Weak
Crazy Thoughts – My Book of Sin
Broken
Ode to Mr. Dean Fraser

A Little Little Talk
A Little Little Talk – Book Two

Prayers
My Collective
A Little Talk/A Time For Fun and Play
Simple Poems
Behind The Scars
Songs of Praise And Love

Love Bound
Love Bound – Book Two

Dedication Unto My Kids
More Talk
Saving America From A Woman's Perspective
My Collective the Other Side of Me
My Collective the Dark Side of Me
A Blessed Day
Lose To Win
My Doubtful Days – Book One

My Little Talk With God
My Little Talk With God – Book Two

A Different Mood and World – Thinking

My Nagging Day
My Nagging Day – Book Two
Friday September 13, 2013
My True Love
It Would Be You
My Day

A Little Advice – Talk
1313, 2032, 2132 – The End of Man
Tata

MICHELLE'S BOOK BLOG – BOOKS 1 – 20

My Problem Day
A Better Way
Stay – Adultery and the Weight of Sin – Cleanliness Message

Let's Talk
Lonely Days – Foundation
A Little Talk With Jamaica – As Long As I Live
Instructions For Death
My Lonely Thoughts
My Lonely Thoughts – Book Two
My Morning Talks – Prayers With God
What A Mess
My Little Book
A Little Word With You
My First Trip of 2015
Black Mother – Mama Africa
Islamic Thought
My California Trip January 2015
My True Devotion by Michelle – Michelle Jean

My Many Questions To God
My Talk